Linda
Demirel

THE CHILDREN'S BOOK OF POTTERY

Christine Rowe

B.T. Batsford Ltd, London

To my former pupils at Holland Park School

First published 1989
© Christine E Rowe 1989

ISBN 0 7134 5995 6

Printed in Great Britain by
The Bath Press, Bath

Contents

Acknowledgements

Most of the pottery in this book was made by the pupils of Holland Park Comprehensive School in London. I thank them for several years of rewarding and creative pleasure in seeing them and their work develop.

Thanks are also due to Rose Kenny – my photographic advisor, Bridget Saunders – for her word processing, Chris Rainsley – Pottery Assistant, and friends and colleagues for their support and encouragement.

Introduction

How to Use This Book

Above all, this book is written to use and enjoy. I hope it will be an encouragement to make as many of the projects as possible. Of course these are not the only solutions, just the ones that these young potters came up with. Don't be afraid to experiment with other ways of making and decorating using clay materials, once you get the idea of what holds together successfully. I suggest you keep a visual diary of your progress as a potter. You could use it to draw ideas for pots, and patterns to put on them, to paste in pictures of pots from magazines and exhibitions and to write yourself notes about pottery facts that you don't want to forget. The local and national museums and art galleries are full of wonderful old and new pots to give you ideas and inspiration about what is possible; some addresses are at the back of the book in 'More Ideas'.

Finally I hope you will find *The Children's Book of Pottery* useful when you want to make pots at home on the kitchen table, or at the youth club where there might be a kiln or space to build a bonfire or a raku kiln, as well as in school, in class or at the pottery club.

Good potting!

Christine

1 Things you will need to have

Clay

This is your most important item and is a natural material. Depending where you live, it may be possible to take a bucket and spade and dig some up from the ground. It is often quite yellow or blue-grey in colour and will need to be picked over carefully to take out any little stones and leaves, etc. It should feel sticky and soft when you squeeze it, a bit like bread dough. You may need to get some help to make sure you have found the right material.

If you would prefer to use ready prepared clay you can usually find it in your local art store, or a nearby working pottery might sell you a small amount.

There is a list of the main suppliers of pottery materials at the end of this book. If you write them a letter they will send you a catalogue of all the latest pottery clays, tools and colours.

Other Things

Anything else you need can usually be found by looking around. Potters have always been good at using what is there.

A table – this should be steady and big enough to work on if you are hand building and to spread out your things.

Cloth – an old linen cloth or hessian sacking is best, to roll out the clay for making slab pots or tiles. It will prevent the clay sticking to the table.

Knife – this should have a thin blade but not be sharp. A kitchen knife is best, with a comfortable handle.

Plastic – a sheet of polythene or a plastic bag, big enough to wrap your work in if you need to keep it damp.

Sponges – a large one for cleaning your table and tools when you have finished using them. A small natural one for smoothing over the clay surface.

Rolling pin – a smooth wooden one – but you cannot then put it back in the kitchen to use for food! A straight-sided bottle would be alright too.

Wire – a cheese wire or a 30 cm (12 in) length of picture hanging wire, with rings at each end to pull tightly for cutting the clay.

Needle – a metal point set into a cork or with a wooden handle.

Slip trailing bulb – for decorating with slip.

Rolling guides – pieces of wood 5 mm ($\frac{1}{5}$ in) thick, 45 cm (18 in) long, for keeping clay the same thickness all over as you flatten it to make slab pots, press-moulded dishes and tiles.

Bowl or bucket – to soak down hard clay.

Clean bricks or a slab of plaster – to drain off the slurry.

Wooden board (a batt) – plain with no varnish on it.

A bag or wooden box – to keep your growing collection of pottery tools in.

Brushes – small ones for painting detailed patterns, big floppy ones for slip and rough ones for using with wax.

Weighing scales – to weigh out the clay and glaze materials.

Plaster moulds – to make big dishes with, like the ones on page 20.

A sieve mop – this is a big brush for using with the sieve, instead of your hands.

Sieves – 80 mesh grade is useful for most jobs and a 200 mesh for glaze materials.

Wooden rib – a shaped piece of wood to help with forming a pot on a wheel.

Potter's wheel – you will need this if you are throwing and turning a pot. You can often find them at school, in local working potteries, a youth centre or you can buy them from art stores or pottery suppliers' catalogues.

Colouring materials – check that you are using non-toxic materials – coloured slips, oxides, glaze materials, glazes, underglaze colours, on-glaze enamels – these can usually be bought safely from a pottery materials supplier, but all you really need to start with is a lump of clay and your potter's thumb.

Health and Safety

Remember not to put any clay materials in your mouth.
Those I have suggested here are not poisonous but it is wise to have good habits.
A potter's enemy is DUST, which is not a problem if you can work outside, but indoors you need to remember:

▷ Sponge everything clean after using it
▷ Wear an apron to keep dust from your clothes
▷ Wash your apron regularly
▷ Don't make dust if you can help it
▷ If you see any dust wipe it up
▷ Don't breath dust in; it's bad for you

If you drop any clay on the floor pick it up before anyone slips on it.

Take care and stay safe!

2 Looking after the clay

If you have bought your clay or are using it in a clay workshop it has already been carefully prepared using a pug mill – a machine for getting clay to feel even and ready to use.

Just before you begin to use the soft (called plastic) clay you should prepare it by wedging or banging it. This is necessary for three main reasons:

▷ to drive out any air bubbles
▷ to get rid of lumps
▷ to take out excess water

Wedge the clay on the table by leaning hard on it and then turning it a little to make a sort of spiral, leaning then turning, leaning then turning until you think no air can be left inside the clay lump. Test it by cutting at the base with your wire. The best way to learn wedging is by watching someone doing it. Who can you find to watch?

Another way to get the air out of the clay is to bang it down hard on the table, then cut it in half with the wire, then bang the two pieces back together a different way, cut and bang, cut and bang until the clay lump is smooth.

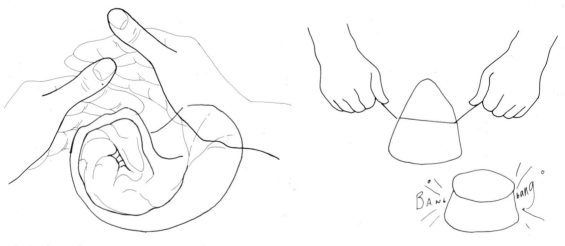

Spiral wedging   *Cut and bang*

Preparing clay takes a lot of energy and it is a marvellous thing to do if you are feeling angry about something because it gives you a chance to really let off steam.

Keeping Your Work Damp

When you are half-way through making something, you may need to keep your pottery damp so that you can finish it another time. You could keep it out of the air which is drying it by:

▷ sealing it inside a plastic tub
▷ wrapping it carefully in polythene
▷ putting it in a damp cupboard

Soaking Down the Clay

Pieces of clay that are too hard to use any more can be covered with water in a bowl or bucket and left overnight to soak. Then pour off the water and drain this resulting slurry on a block of plaster, or some clean bricks or an old wooden table, until it is ready to wedge and use again. It only takes a matter of hours, depending on the weather, particularly if it is outside. This way none of the clay is wasted and as long as it is still clean it can be used over and over again until it is ready to fire in the kiln. These piles of slurry in the picture are draining on a table ready for wedging tomorrow. What sort of pots are the girls making?

3 Hand building

To Make a Pinch Pot

You will be using your thumb, so it is
sometimes called a thumb pot.

 You will need:
▷ a piece of clay the size of a tennis ball
▷ a potter's needle
▷ your best thumb, without a long nail on it

1. Roll the clay into a very even, smooth
   ball. You could do this between your
   two hands or on the table.

2. Stick your thumb into the middle of
   the clay ball.

3. Pinch the clay between your thumb
   and fingers.

4. Continue pinching all the way round
   until you have made a small bowl.
   If you have used grogged clay this
   could be used in the raku firing
   shown on page 56 or these pots from
   David's drawing of a slice of orange.

5. If you can make two bowls the same
   size and join them rim to rim, you
   could make the pigs on page 12 and
   the hairy animals on page 45, or use
   these examples to make your own
   animals, real or imaginary.

To Make a Pottery Pig

Make two pinch pot bowls into an egg.

Put a blob of clay on for his nose.

Make two nostrils in the nose with your
  needle.

Make two piggy eye holes with your
  needle.

Put four blobs of clay underneath for
  his feet.

Put two flat ears pointing down
  – and don't forget a curly coiled
  worm for the tail.

Let him dry, then biscuit fire him, and
  he is yours forever.

To Make a Coil pot

Making pots with snakes

You will need:

▷ a lump of wedged clay
▷ a wooden board
▷ a natural sponge

1. Make a ball of clay and flatten it onto the wooden board until it is as thick as your little finger.

2. Take a piece of clay the size of a sausage and roll it with both hands to make a snake about as thick as your little finger.

3. Build the sides up by coiling the snake round and round. Press the clay snake in place as you go with your thumbs.

4. Every three or four rows smooth down with your thumb on the inside and the outside, to make it really strong.

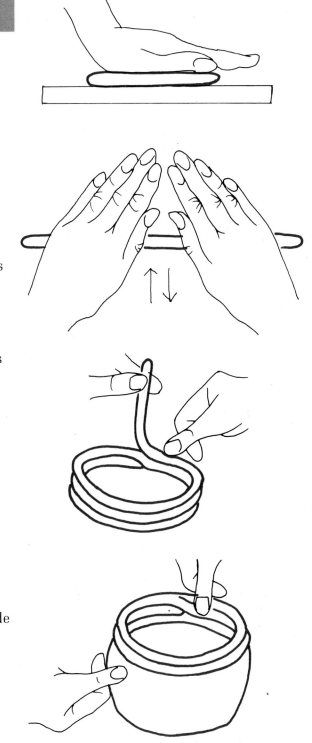

Hand building

Younger children made these coil pots by first looking at trees, then drawing them and spelling out the different parts of a tree. Start by coiling the trunk, then divide it to make branches and divide them to make twigs.

Trunks
Branches
twigs

African calabash were Em's inspiration for these two coiled bowls with incised decoration. Calabash are the dried outside part of gourds that grow in Africa and the Caribbean. Coiling is one of the oldest ways we know of making pottery. For the most wonderful examples look for water pots made by the women in many parts of Africa and the decorated bowls of the Pueblo Indians in New Mexico.

These are examples of different ways of using the coiling method of making pots with snakes. Once you are able to build your pot strong enough to hold together there is no limit to the size you could make it. If the pot starts to feel wobbly and unsafe, leave it to become a little firmer. If this means leaving it overnight or longer, make sure to put damp cloths and plastic on the top edge so that it stays as soft as the new clay you will add on when you continue building. You can gently beat a coil pot into a more regular, even shape using a flat stick if it starts to get too uneven. You can scrape a leather hard (nearly dry) coil pot thinner and make it more even at the same time if need be.

Jake (*right*) is coiling a very large pot ▷ in sections so that it will fit into the kiln. The parts are separated with strips of newspaper in between while they are drying to prevent sticking.

The coils for this planter were placed in their own pattern and only smoothed over on the inside for strength.

Bridgette has added a strong handle ▷ made with two coils pressed side by side to make this tall jug. She polished over some of the coils to emphasise the built-in pattern.

1/ you wedge the clay THEN

GET CLAY and flatten it with a rolling pin.

SLAB~POT
HOW TO MAKE A SLAB-POT

3/ Then you get a knife and cut out a shape

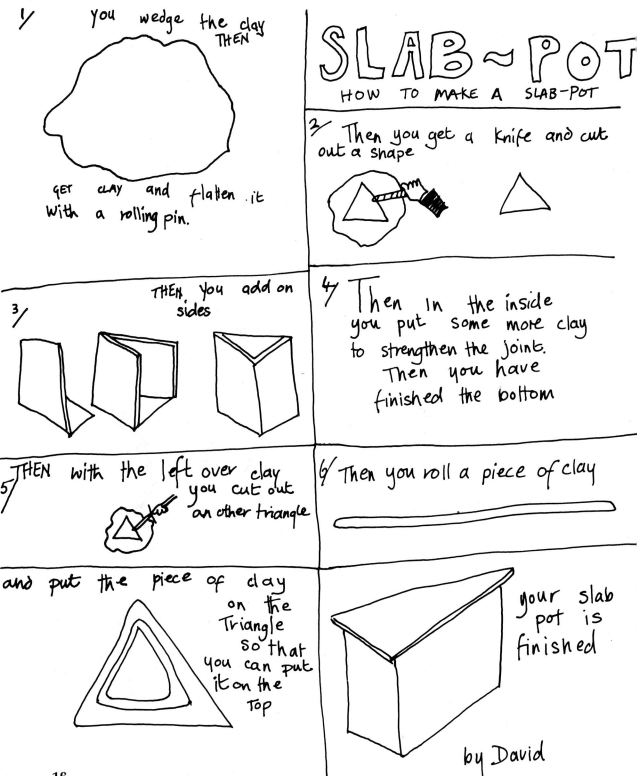

3/ THEN you add on sides

4/ Then In the inside you put some more clay to strengthen the joint. Then you have finished the bottom

5/ THEN with the left over clay you cut out an other triangle

6/ Then you roll a piece of clay

and put the piece of clay on the Triangle so that you can put it on the Top

your slab pot is finished

by David

16

This Is Where You Need the Rolling Pin

David shows you in a comic strip how to make a triangular pot with a simple lid. Verona below is making a pyramid pot from her templates (paper patterns) so that she gets the sides the right sizes. You will get a neater result if you do this as well, although it may seem like extra trouble to start with. When you roll out the clay use two rolling guides or sticks of the same thickness. Put them each side of the clay and keep rolling until the clay is the same thickness all over as the sticks. You will find it easier if you roll out the clay on a cloth to prevent it sticking to the table, and keep turning the clay over so that you roll both sides. This is a bit like rolling out pastry, pasta dough or chapatis and will help you develop good strong muscles. Let the clay stiffen until it is leather hard before you use the templates to cut out the shapes, then join them together using slurry and a roll of clay like this:

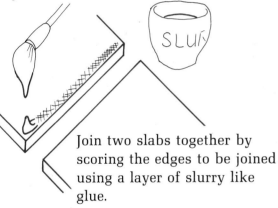

Join two slabs together by scoring the edges to be joined using a layer of slurry like glue.

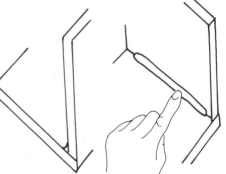

Press in a thin roll of clay to seal the crack and strengthen the joint.

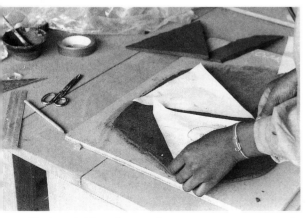

Cut out the clay using paper templates.

Join the sides one by one, making the joins neat with a roll of clay.

A Tall Vase With a Lacy Pattern

See the colour photo between pages 48 and 49 showing Una with her pot, made by bending the clay round to make a tube, or cylinder. She made it after looking closely at the patterns on a piece of lace or crochet work.

You will need:

▷ linen or sacking to roll out the clay
▷ a piece of lacy material
▷ a potter's knife
▷ a cardboard tube, like those inside carpets, covered with newspaper to prevent the clay sticking. (A shop that sells carpets would let you have these)
▷ some slurry and a brush to put it on with

1. Roll out a piece of light coloured clay on a cloth.
2. Spread a piece of lace over the top and roll that over, pressing it into the clay with the rolling pin.
3. Wrap the clay round a cardboard tube covered in newspaper to make a tall cylinder supported by the tube, joined down the side.
4. Cut one edge straight and stand that edge onto another rolled out piece of clay.
5. Cut this round for the base and carefully join it onto the cylinder by modelling it with a finger or wooden tool.
6. Carefully take off the lace, then slide out the cardboard tube. Don't worry about the newspaper, it can burn off in the kiln.
7. After bisque (the first) firing, glaze with a coloured transparent glaze that will run into the design to emphasise it.

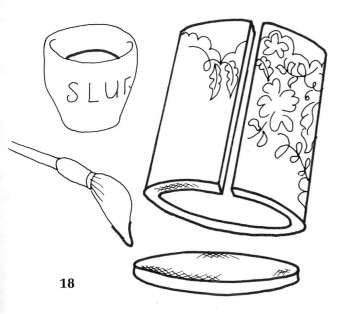

Pat has made a tall slab pot using the ▷ shape of a chinese pagoda. The photograph was taken before it went into the kiln so that you can see more clearly how it was made. She made each section separately, then stacked them up as the Han dynasty Chinese potters used to do in AD 500.

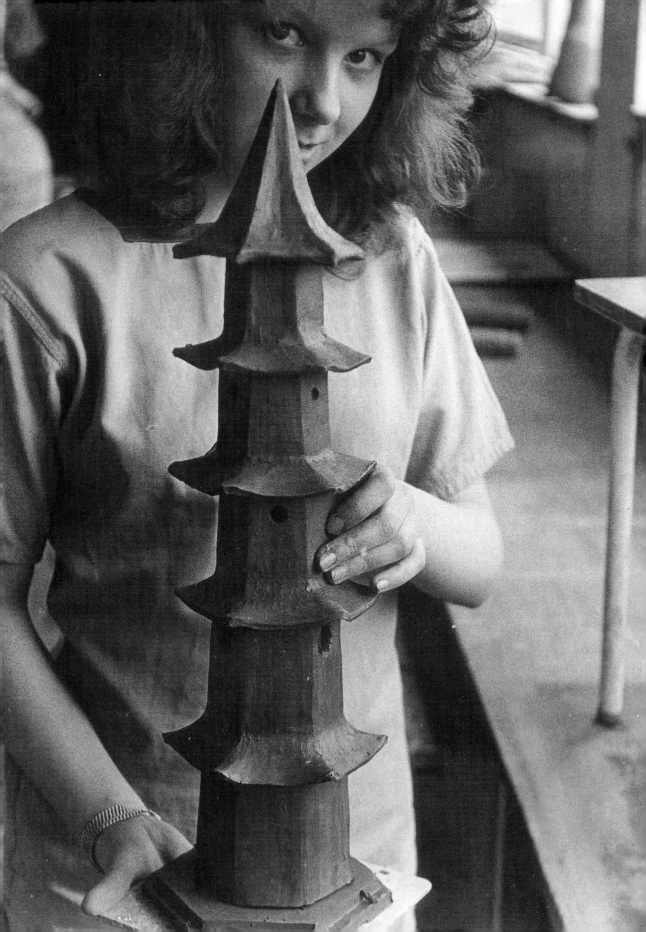

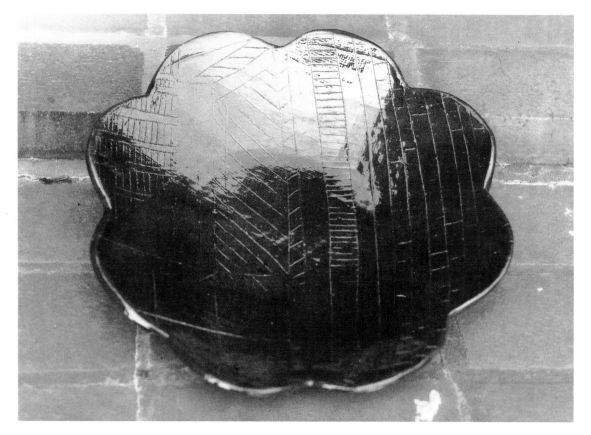

This dish has an incised pattern scratched in with a potter's needle and has been glazed with a rich shiny stoneware glaze called 'tenmoku'. (The glaze recipe is given on page 49.)

Below are two types of moulds, the one we used here and another hump, or mushroom-shaped, mould. They are made from plaster of Paris.

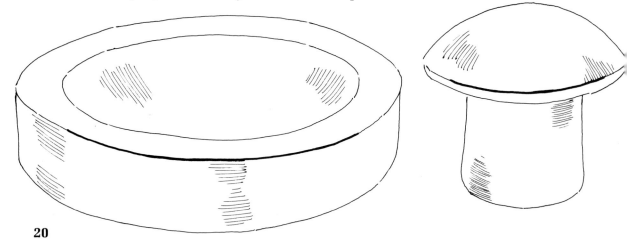

Using a Mould

A simple way to make a large dish

You will need:

▷ a rolling pin
▷ rolling guides
▷ a natural sponge
▷ a plaster mould
▷ a piece of cloth
▷ wire to cut the clay
▷ a tablespoon

Roll out the clay on the cloth, using the rolling guides to keep the clay the same thickness.

Lift it with the cloth still underneath if it is a large piece of clay and place it into a dry plaster mould. Take care not to stretch the clay at the base but ease it in gently from the sides.

Dampen a natural sponge and use it to smooth gently over the surface of the dish until there are no more bumps or dents. After a few hours the clay will be leather hard and you can take it out of the mould. Do this by placing a board over the top and turning the whole thing upside down, then lifting off the plaster mould. You will need a friend to help you do this.

While the dish is upside down you could polish it with a tablespoon, but you might prefer the pattern that is left by the cloth you used for rolling out the clay.

Now turn the dish over and cut the edge to your design, then round off the rim with the damp sponge so that there are no sharp bits. If you want a straight, even rim, cut it while it is in the mould using the top of the mould as a guide for your knife or wire. Now it is ready to scratch in a pattern before drying, biscuit firing and glazing.

4 Throwing and turning or making pots on a potter's wheel; trimming their bases

This series of pictures shows Patrick making a pot on a potter's wheel. This way of making is called *Throwing*, because as the wheel head spins round it tries to throw the clay off. You could see this happening if you put some water on the wheel head then spun the wheel round. The water would quickly fly off.

When you throw a pot on the wheel it is the sticky, plastic clay and the potter's hands that control it to shape a simple ball of clay into a beautiful bowl.

Start by wedging the clay carefully and patting it into a round ball. Press the ball onto the middle of the dry wheelhead using the rings marked on it to guide you. Make sure you are standing or sitting comfortably and leaning on your arms to steady them. Now wet the clay and your hands to help them run over the clay and *Centre* the clay while the wheel is going round quite fast, until it has a flat top and straight sides. When it looks still and centred, press your thumbs slowly into the middle of the lump to make a *Well*. The slower you do this to start with the more likely it is that the well will be in the middle. Judge carefully how deep the hole will be so that you leave at least a centimetre of clay for the bottom of the pot. With your thumb and fingers, as Patrick shows you, gently squeeze the side of the pot; this is called *Pulling up*, so that it is an even thickness all round. Finish off the *Rim* of the pot with your sponge for neatness and smoothness. If the top becomes uneven you could trim it off with the needle by slowly pressing it through the clay and lifting off the uneven top. If the pot is too thick and uneven at the bottom you could trim it using a wooden rib to tidy it up and to alter the shape if you wished. Take any water out of the bottom of the pot with your sponge while the wheel is still going round. When it all looks good to you, stop the wheel, flood a little water onto the wheelhead and cut underneath the pot with your cutting wire until the pot is floating. Slide it gently off the wheel and on to your hand and then a wooden board or *Batt*. The cross-section of the pot shows how evenly thin this needs to be.

When you have cut the pot off the wheel leave it to dry until it is leather hard; that is, stiff but not dry. Turn it upside down and fix it back on the wheel again with four sausages of the same colour clay, ready for the next process, which is *Turning* or neatening up the uneven bottom of the pot.

Your first pots may look like these, but keep practising. Use your best experiments to test all the glazes and colours that are available to you where you are making them. Make lots of bowls and cylinders and you will soon be able to make some of the other thrown pots illustrated in this book.

Throwing Tips

▷ Make your ball of clay as round as possible before it goes into the wheel, then your work is nearly done

▷ Keep your hands wet so that the clay can run smoothly through them without sticking

▷ Sit very still while you are throwing and lean on your arms to steady them. Your hands must stay in the same shape for at least one whole turn of the wheel if the pot is to stay well centred and even

▷ Try to make the wall of the pot evenly thin from the bottom to the rim at the top

▷ Finish each pull up with a slight pressure down on the rim to steady it

▷ Use a natural sponge fixed to a stick to mop out any water that collects inside a tall pot so that you can always see the bottom

▷ Find experienced potters and watch them for as long as you can and as often as you can to pick up the best throwing tips

Turning Tools

Here are some examples of turning tools you may come across. The top one has been carved by a Japanese potter, the middle ones you can usually buy in an art store. The bottom one you could make yourself with a piece of wood for the handle, 15 cm (6 in) of metal strip, four nails to hold it in place and a piece of string to bind it all together.

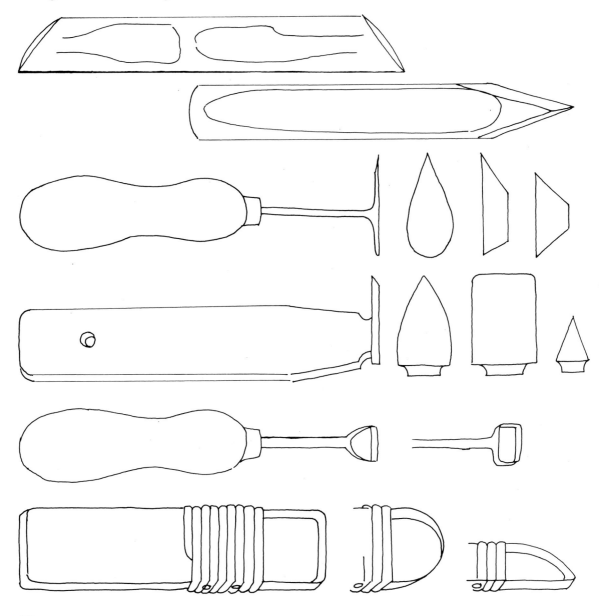

Chris Demonstrating Turning

Centre the pot using the rings on the wheel head and test with a finger that it is centred.

Fix the pot down with your thumb and four sausages of clay.

Steady your arms by leaning on the rubber rim and flatten the top (which is really the bottom!).

Trim away the uneven bits and thin the sides where they are thick.

Make a dip in the middle if the clay is thick enough. The raised bit that is left is called the *Foot*.

The finished thrown and turned bowl, ready for drying evenly upside down and then biscuit firing.

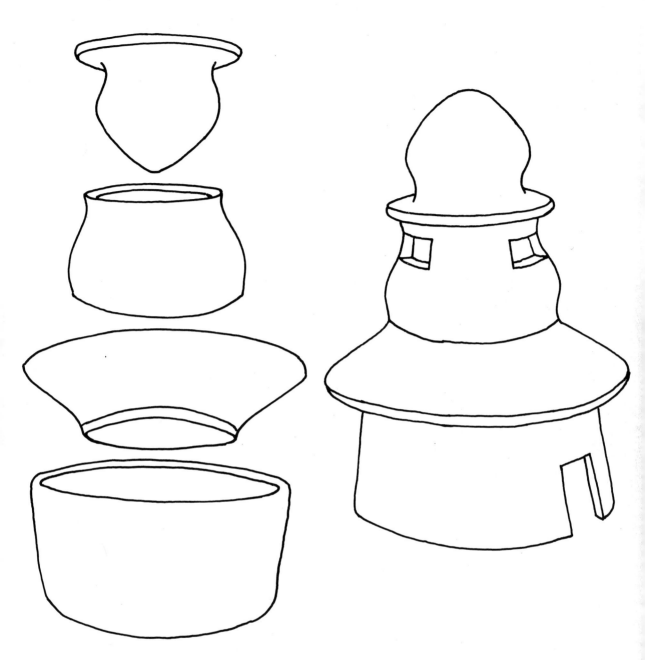

Duc Vu made these and put them together like this to make a temple

He turned the little pots when they were leather hard and then decided how to rearrange them.

He cut holes in some of the pots so that air would not be trapped inside the finished temple, which could have made firing difficult.

He fixed the parts together with slurry as if it was a slab pot and finished by turning over the joins and sponging them until they were invisible.

Designing a Mug

There are several things you will need to think about when you are designing a mug with a handle.

The rim
▷ It should feel very smooth to your lips
▷ It should be wide enough to put your hand in to clean it

Handle
▷ Not too high so that it knocks onto the draining board when you wash it and put it upside down to drain
▷ Place it opposite the main weight of the liquid
▷ Don't have it too far from the bowl so it is strong enough
▷ It should seem to grow out of the mug like a branch of a tree

Bottom
▷ It needs to be smooth so that it sits squarely on the table

Sides
▷ They should be fairly straight, so that you can drink the last drop of coffee without standing on your head

Not Like This

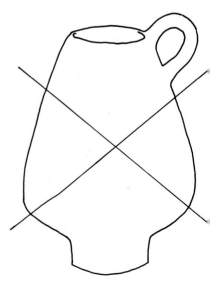

How many design faults can you spot? It may look elegant but is it practical to use? Of course you might decide to make a sculpture that was a mug because it was hollow, had a handle, a foot and a lip, but was totally disguised as something else. That could be wonderful too.

Ronit's Mugs

These are thrown and turned bowls with pulled handles as shown here.

Take a pear-sized piece of clay, wet it and stroke it downwards, changing the position of your hand around with each stroke, from facing left to facing right, until the clay is long enough to make a handle.

Fix it on to the side of the pot after you have turned it. Press the top of the handle on first and bend it round your fingers to get a good shape, then press on the bottom part and finish it by neatening with your sponge.

Look carefully at the handles of the cups and mugs in your kitchen at home. Draw some of them and decide which are the best ones, the most comfortable to hold and easy to use. Ronit did all that research before she designed these mugs.

31

This was made in a plaster mould, polished smooth with the back of a spoon, decorated on the inside and the outside with impressed and incised decoration and glazed with a rich, shiny glaze to give a watery finish.

Animal tiles set in glass

Can you spot which are glaze-rimmed pinch pots and which are tree fungus found in the park? It is often useful to look carefully at nature for your design.

Two pinch pots are put together to make a hollow form and then decorated with trailed slip to make these cactus pots. Don't forget to put in a little hole somewhere to let out the air inside before the pot is fired in the kiln. If you don't it will blow up as the air inside expands with the heat.

5 Decorating pottery

In this part of the book different ways of decorating the surface of pottery are described. Of course you can combine the different ways as well, as this crocodile dish shows.

Find ideas for patterns and motifs in your scrapbook, visual diary and from patterns and shapes that you see around you. Use your imagination as well and find ideas from simply playing or doodling with the tools and materials suggested here. There is a list on page 47 of the different ways of decorating that are described, but I expect you can invent other ways as well.

Impressed Decoration

While the clay is still soft, press shapes into it. The crocodile dish used a pencil point to make the scales, circle and rim of the dish. You could press buttons, leaves, shells, nuts and bolts, lace, fingers, etc. into the clay to build up a pattern. These tiles were pressed from shoe soles.

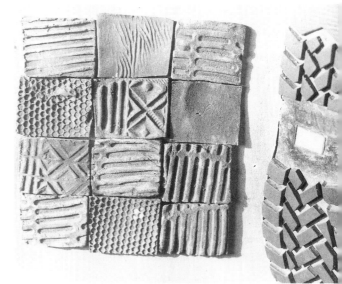

Incised Decoration

When the clay is leather hard press a line into it, taking care not to leave any crumbs of clay on the surface. (You can sweep these away with a dry paintbrush.) After biscuit firing use a glaze that runs into the pattern.

This pattern was doodled while Caryl was thinking about cobwebs.

Sgraffitto

This is an Italian word that sounds a little bit like scratching, which is exactly what you do. When the surface of the clay has been decorated using sgraffitto one layer of material has been scratched through to show another colour underneath. The sgraffitto may be made through slip coloured with oxides onto the clay or through oxides onto glaze.

How to do it
Make a dish in a mould, using terracotta clay – the brown, earthenware clay.

Cover the inside with a smooth layer of white slip, which you may have to sieve to get out any tiny lumps.

Wait until the shine disappears from the slip and it becomes leather hard; that is, stiff but not dry.

With a needle draw a pattern or picture, write a message or a poem, pressing just hard enough so that you can see the dark colour of the clay showing clearly through. The two dishes above were painted with slip and the patterns on the snake scratched through with a needle.

Jake used this method to make his cartoon dish.

Inlay Decoration

In this method of decoration the design is first incised and then the hole is filled in with another colour.

   This set of beakers was decorated after looking at the paintings of Matisse. If you can find some pictures of his work you will see what inspired Ella.

1. Take balls of clay all of the same size and try to throw each one using the same hand movements, so that they are same shape.
2. When they are turned, incise the decoration, then inlay it with a contrasting colour of clay or slip. For instance, terracotta inlaid with white slip, or grey clay inlaid with terracotta.
3. Wait until the inlay is leather hard, then scrape or turn over the top to make a smooth, even surface.
4. Glaze with a transparent earthenware glaze to bring out the maximum contrast or difference between the body and the decoration.

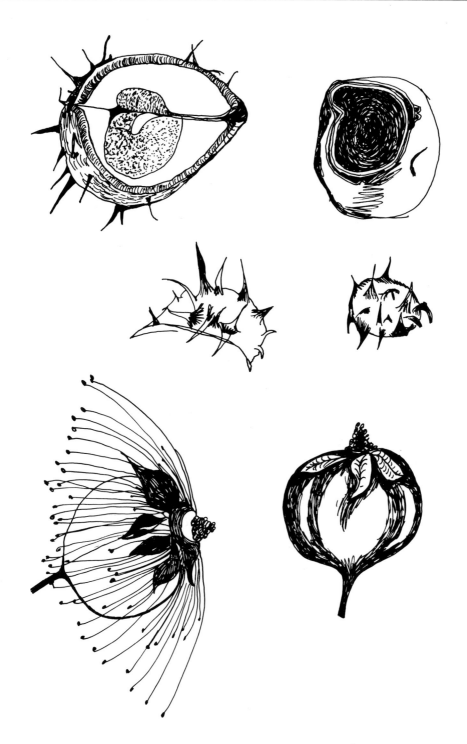

Preparing Slip

You will need:

▷ two basins
▷ two wooden sticks
▷ a sieve
▷ a sieve mop
▷ dry powdered clay
▷ slip stain
▷ water to mix

Slip is made of clay, water and a colouring oxide or slip stain. You can buy it ready made or you can prepare it yourself. You will have to make sure that the slip you want to use is suitable for the clay that you have; they must fuse together on your pot through firing. The person to ask is the one who is supplying your materials. The amount of stain to use will be in the supplier's catalogue.

If you are preparing the slip from a dry powder, start by putting the water into a basin or bucket so that you don't make too much dust fly into the air for you to breathe in; remember that is not safe practice for potters. Next add the slip powder, stirring it to make it smooth and creamy. Then put your hands in and squeeze out as many lumps as possible.

When all this is reasonably smooth and about as thin as custard, sieve it through a sieve graded about 80 mesh. Put two sticks across the basin to balance the sieve on so that all the drips are caught.

Help it through the sieve with a brush called a sieve mop, taking care just to stroke the sieve mesh as it is delicate and breaks easily. Try to get all the lumps through the sieve, adding more water if you need to.

The smooth slip in the basin is now ready to use for lining a dish, dipping into, slip trailing or painting on to a leather hard pot.

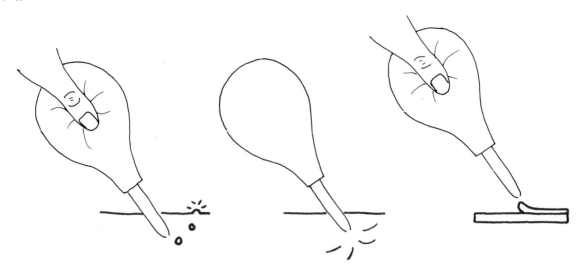

Squeeze the air
out of the slip trailer

Suck in the
smooth slip

Slowly squirt it
out on to the clay surface

Slip trailing using a bulb
Nasrin was inspired in her biology
class to make this coil pot like a sticky
bud and decorate it with slip trailing in
several colours. Look at the colour
photograph of the cactus pot which has
also been decorated with trailed slip.
The pottery cactus has been hidden in a
bowl of real ones because the pattern
was copied from them.

Tile Panel for a Classroom Sink Splashback

You will need:

▷ clay and glaze
▷ cloth and rolling pin
▷ tile cutter, or template and knife
▷ slip trailer and slip

Skills required

▷ rolling out clay
▷ using the tile cutter or cutting round a template
▷ squeezing a slip trailer and making patterns
▷ spreading the tile cement

After examining the space around the sink, measure up and decide how many tiles will be needed. Remember that clay shrinks about ten per cent so you will have to allow for that in your calculations.

1. Roll out some clay on a cloth.
2. Cut out the tiles from a template or use a tile cutter.
3. Decide on a method of decoration. (We looked at sliced fruit to make slip trailed patterns of the seeds inside.)
4. Fire and glaze the tiles. We used honey earthenware glaze (recipe on page 49).
5. Fix in place with tile cement and grout the spaces in between.

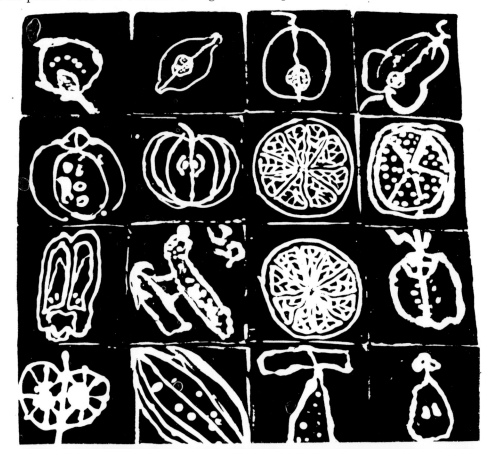

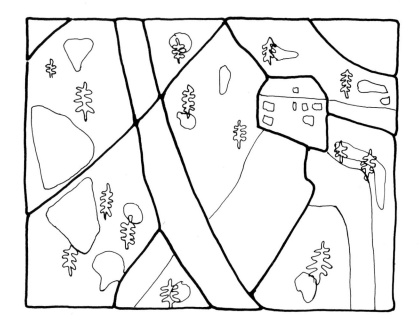

Slip Painting

Edward's panel

You will need several colours of slip to paint this decorative picture.

Roll out a large slab of clay and cut it to the shape of the finished panel.

You can start painting it straight away and keep adding different colours of clay and wiping them off while the clay is still leather hard. Put the slip on with big floppy brushes or your fingers.

When the design is finished, no longer wet, and the clay is leather hard, cut up the panel carefully. Make the cut out shapes follow the lines of the design, the size not bigger than about 20 cm (8 in) in any direction.

Turn the jigsaw pieces upside down on to clean newsprint and leave them to dry slowly under a wooden board so that the edges don't curl up.

Biscuit fire and glaze the pieces separately with a clear, transparent glaze them when they come out of the kiln, then mount them on to a wooden board with a frame.

Marbled Dishes

You will need:

▷ a plaster mould
▷ several colours of slip
▷ a knife or wire to cut the edges
▷ a cloth and rolling pin
▷ rolling guides
▷ a slip trailing bulb

1. Roll out a slab of clay a little bigger than the size of the plaster mould and fit it carefully inside.
2. Trim the edges evenly and sponge over the surface so that it is smooth.
3. Line the dish with smooth sieved slip.
4. Trail other colours of slip over this surface while it is still wet, using the trailing bulb.

Quickly pick up the mould and shake it a little so that the slips mix up together and create a marbled effect.

Now let it dry to leather hard before taking out of the mould and fettling the edges. Biscuit fire and glaze with a clear glaze.

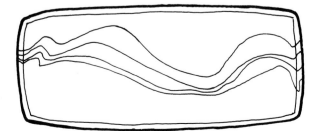

Applied Decoration

If your throwing is progressing well you
might try these flower pots or planters
with faces.

Throw and turn the pots. Flatten one
side by gently tapping on the table and
put in two holes so that it can hang up.

Make coils and press them on well,
with two blobs for eyes and longer bits
for noses and smiles, as Ella's pots show
you here.   ▷

Modelling a Portrait Head

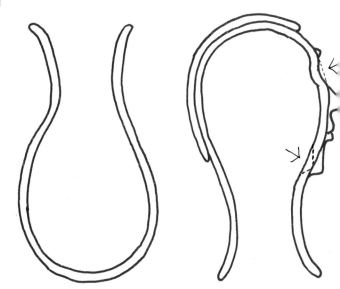

You will need:

▷ clay for coiling
▷ a turntable or small board to work on
▷ polythene to wrap up the pot until it is finished
▷ a friend to model from or a mirror

Skills required

▷ to make a fairly large (or small) vase-shaped coil pot
▷ to recognise the difference between how people look
▷ to model features confidently
▷ to use a modelling tool if required

Portrait heads

After drawing the portrait of a friend (or of yourself in the mirror):

1. Make a vase-shaped coil pot with narrower top.
2. When this is leather hard, turn it upside down to be the basic head form.
3. Add on to this extra clay for the nose, chin, hair and other features.
4. Try to make it look as much like yourself or your friend, as you can, as Harmeesh has managed to do with his friend. I think he has got his smile just right and that shows good observation. If you turn the page upside down you can probably see the sort of vase shape that had to be made to start with.
5. Dry the pot very carefully and fire it without a glaze so that none of the modelling is covered up. A sawdust firing or bonfire kiln might be the most suitable.

Modelling Monsters

Start off with a sausage-sized piece of clay.

Pinch it to make scales on its back.

Add on four legs, or more!

Your own monster could have a long tail, lots of teeth, big eyes, long claws on its feet, a forked tongue, pointed ears and anything you can think of to make it seem more scary.

If any part of the monster ends up thicker than your thumb then make little holes underneath to help it in the firing.

Teresa shows you some of her dinosaurs above.

Hairy Animals

A cat and dog from thumb pots

You will need:

▷ a ball of clay
▷ an old sieve or tea strainer
▷ a wooden board to work on
▷ some slurry
▷ a knife

Make a ball of clay the size of a tennis ball.

Cut it in half and use the two halves to make pinch pot bowls with the same size rims.

Join the two bowls together, rim to rim, as in the diagrams on pages 11 and 12 for the birds.

Make ears that stick up for the cat and ones that hang down for the dog.

Push pellets of clay through the sieve to make hair and scrape it off gently with a knife before applying it to your animal.

Paint slurry where you want the hair to stick and gently press it into place.

Impress the eyes, nose and mouth.

Oxide Painting and Wax

Coil a lovely big pot like this one made by Paul. He cut out a lid and made a strap handle for the top. The outside was smoothed very carefully then the pot was dried and biscuit fired. After the firing he mixed some different coloured oxides with liquid wax and painted them on to the biscuit pot like big leaves. When the oxides are first painted on, of course, they look black because they need the heat of the kiln and the action of the glaze to bring out the colours.

> Cobalt oxide becomes blue to black
> Copper oxide becomes green to black
> Iron oxide becomes yellow to grey

As soon as the wax was dry, he dipped part of the pot in a light-coloured stoneware glaze. The wax resisted the glaze and made the unusual textures that you see here. During the stoneware firing the wax completely burnt away leaving an oxide and glaze pattern.

Decoration Summary

How and when to put pattern on to the pot

Before biscuit firing:

impressed
incised
inlay
sgraffitto
slip trailing
marbling
applied decoration
modelling
plus combinations of any of these. (All methods are described in the projects.)

After biscuit firing:

WAX – paint the pot with liquid wax before dipping in the glaze
OXIDES – paint on the different colours mixed with water
– rub them on dry with a cloth
– wash them on thinly with lots of water so that the oxide collects in the dips of your patterns
– splash and flick them on top of the glaze
MELTED GLASS – use smashed glass but remember the retaining wall to hold the melted glass in place
UNDERGLAZE COLOURS – mix with the medium to paint before glazing
– mix with water to paint or splash and spatter on top of the glaze
– buy them in crayons and scribble with them
GLAZES – scratch through the glaze to show the body colour; trail one glaze on top of another like slip
– splash or paint contrasting colours on top of one another

After glaze firing:

LUSTRES – paint them on and refire at about 750°C (1382°F)
STENCILS – cut out the coloured shapes and make them permanent by refiring to the temperature on the packet
ON-GLAZE ENAMELS – mix with fat oil and thin with turpentine and use like oil paint
– press them or spatter through a stencil

Animal Tiles

You will need:

▷ stoneware clay
▷ kitchen knife
▷ rolling pin
▷ cloth to roll clay out
▷ broken glass (coloured wine bottles)

After a visit to the zoo, a look at some good animal pictures, slides or films, try your hand at melted glass tiles.

1. Roll out a thin slab of clay and trim to shape.
2. Add on clay to form the animals.
3. Trim the slab of clay to size.
4. Border the clay tile with a pressed on coil.
5. Fill the background with crushed bottle glass.
6. Fire to at least 1100°C (2012°F) to melt the glass thoroughly.

Gloria's smiling tiger (top left) is coloured with a pinch of copper oxide over plain glass, but you could use wine or beer bottles. Can you spot which animals are shown here?

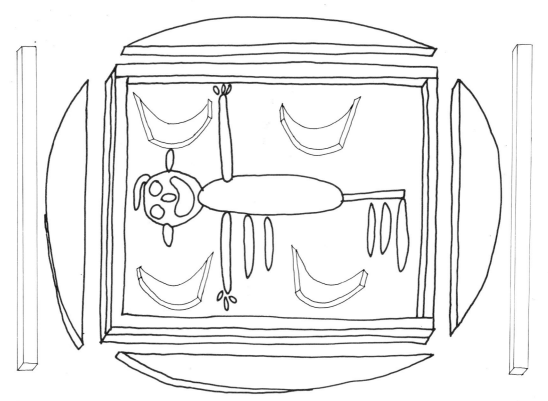

Above: Here is Una with the cylindrical pot she made.
The clay was rolled out on a piece of lace to give the pot its
impressed decoration. See page 18 for the way to make one
just like this.

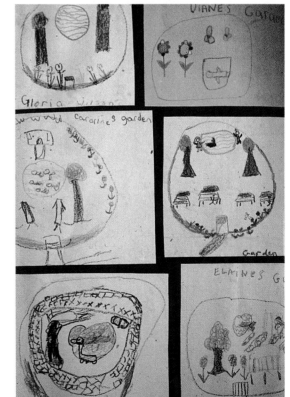

Right: Designs for miniature gardens
*Roll out a piece of clay the shape of your garden design and
build walls with coils. Make a pond from a glazed pinch pot.
After biscuit firing fill the garden with earth and plant with
orange and lemon pips, mustard and cress, tiny clay
sculptures and some cactus, as suggested here. Don't forget
to water it!*

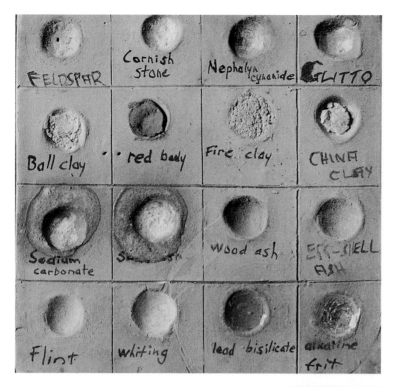

A test showing how individual chemicals have reacted to the heat of the kiln.

Try testing things like sugar, egg shells, scouring powder, finger nails, pins, etc. and see how they react to the kiln.

FELDSPAR

Cornish Stone

Nepholyn cynanide

GLITTO

Ball clay

red body

Fire clay

CHINA CLAY

Sodium carbonate

S. ash

Wood ash

EGG-SHELL ASH

Flint

Whiting

lead bisilicate

alkaline frit

Six traditional glazes for the recipes given

for stoneware:
tenmoku
pebble
celadon

for earthenware:
honey
majolica
clear

6 Glazing: sealing the pottery surface

Glazes can be shiny or matt, earthenware or stoneware, transparent or opaque. They are a form of glass made into a liquid with water so that you can coat your pots with it. The heat of the kiln melts them until they are rather like honey, setting as the kiln cools.

You can buy glazes ready made or in powder form to mix with water like the slip on page 37. Or you can make up a glaze from these recipes with these ingredients from your clay suppliers. (The numbers are parts.)

Clear earthenware	
Lead bisilicate	74
Ball clay	13
Flint	9
Whiting	4
Bentonite	2

Honey earthenware	
Lead bisilicate	100
Dry red clay	35

Majolica earthenware	
Lead bisilicate	38.4
Borax frit	19.7
Tin oxide	4
Zinc oxide	8
China clay	14

Celadon stoneware	
Feldspar	40
Flint	30
Whiting	20
China clay	10
Iron oxide	4

Tenmoku stoneware	
Cornish stone	88
Whiting	12
Iron oxide	8

Pebble stoneware	
China clay	25
Potash feldspar	50
Whiting	5

Make a Glaze

Before you use a glaze for the first time you should test it to see how it comes out in your pottery workshop and with your materials.

1. Collect together the things you need.

the glaze recipe	a damp sponge
and the ingredients	a jam jar with a lid
a small bowl	a spoon
weighing scales	a stiff bristled brush
a 200 mesh sieve	a pen
a sticky label	a biscuit-fired test tile or pinch pot

2. Write the ingredients on the label and stick it on to the jam jar.
3. Put about 2 cm of water into the jam jar and measure out the ingredients in grams into it. Tick them off as you put them in to avoid making a mistake, because most of them will look like the same white powder.
4. Mix up this creamy liquid until it is smooth – you may have to add more water – then sieve all of it gently through the sieve into the bowl. Now check the thickness of the glaze by adding water till it is like thin cream, or by pouring away water from the top if it is too thin.
5. Now dip in the test tile, clean off the base with the damp sponge and place it in the kiln to fire. If you are testing several glazes you will need to remember to make a mark on the back of each test so that you know which one it was when it comes out of the kiln. You can use oxide for this.
6. If this glaze test fires satisfactorily then make up a bucket of glaze using larger amounts with the same proportion of ingredients. You should test this bucket too before you use it, as a check that the recipe was made up correctly.

Now Glaze Your Pot

Where you hold the pot will probably leave finger marks in the wet glaze so only use two fingers to do this.

Dip your pot in the glaze to get one smooth, even layer for only as long as it takes to say 'Straight in, straight out and shake off the drips'.

If there is not enough glaze in the bucket to dip your pot all over you can pour it evenly over the surface with a jug. Fill the inside first and pour it out so that the whole inside is covered. Refill the jug and pour the glaze quickly and evenly over the outside.

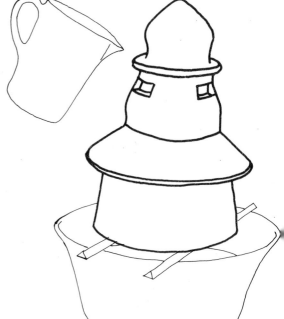

Don't forget to wipe the glaze off cleanly from the bottom of your pot with a damp sponge so that it doesn't stick to the kiln shelves. Sponge a few millimetres ($\frac{1}{4}$ in) up the sides as well in case the glaze runs down too far.

7 Firing pottery in a kiln: rather like cooking

Your school may well have a kiln for firing pottery like the one illustrated here. It uses electricity, but some kilns use gas, oil or wood. You must prepare the clay carefully for the kiln by drying it very well and making sure, as mentioned before, that there are no pockets of air or air bubbles trapped inside any part of the pot. If there are, the air inside them will expand with the heat and pop during firing.

The pots are carefully stacked on shelves rather like a three-dimensional jigsaw, so that every bit of space is taken up inside. If it is glaze firing, lots of care is taken so that pots don't touch one another inside the kiln. Just as the glaze sticks onto the pot during the firing, so it would stick pots together if they were to touch; this is called kissing. If any glaze is left on the bottom of the pot it would stick the pot onto the kiln shelf and might break when you try to unstick it.

For a biscuit firing this is not so important so you would expect to see pots stacked up on top of each other. Plates would have sand in between and underneath them, while pots of the same size could be stacked rim to rim and foot to foot, as long as the stack was steady.

The kiln, or furnace is lined with firebricks or heat resistant fibre to keep the heat inside. The temperature inside the kiln can be controlled by a pyrometer, which shows heat as it builds up past red hot: above 1000°C (1832°F) for earthenware glazes and to about 1250°C (2282°F) for stoneware glazes. It may take all day to slowly build up this amount of heat and overnight to cool enough to be opened.

If you are interested in kilns and firing you could find out about the dragon kilns of China, the bonfire kilns of Africa or the bottle kilns of Staffordshire in England shown here, well as the sawdust and raku firings on the next few pages.

Firing pottery in a kiln: rather like cooking

This is how to start building a sawdust firing using bricks. See how to build the next layer from the pictures. To make nine layers you will need to have 90 bricks, so make sure you have enough. Choose a flat surface to build the kiln on, like plain earth which will not mind the heat.

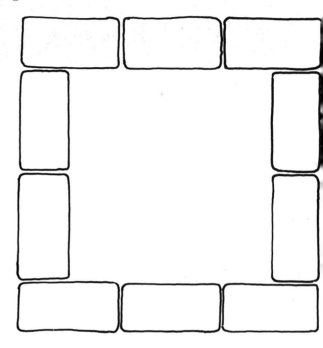

This is an inside view of the sawdust kiln with the pots packed inside and outside with sawdust. Bigger pots are placed at the bottom so that they don't crush the little ones. As the sawdust burns out, the pots will gradually become settled into a heap at the bottom of the kiln. Then the firing is completed.

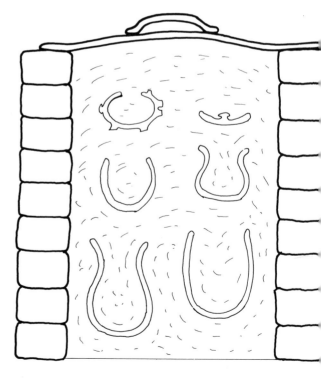

Sawdust Firing

This method of firing can be used in any open space where it is alright to make lots of smoke. Choose a safe place to build your sawdust kiln where it won't disturb anybody if it goes on working for a long time.

You will need:

▷ 90 bricks or a metal bin with holes in the side and a lid
▷ enough sawdust to fill the inside
▷ some dry pots made in a grogged clay
▷ matches

Put the firing together as the drawings show with the sawdust inside and around all the pots, leaving spaces between the bricks for the air to get in so that it doesn't stop burning. Cover the top with a metal lid to douse the flames and leave it to burn through slowly and fire the pots to a mottled black. This might take all day, depending on the size and quality of the sawdust you have been able to find. Don't hurry it; the longer the firing takes the stronger your pots are likely to be.

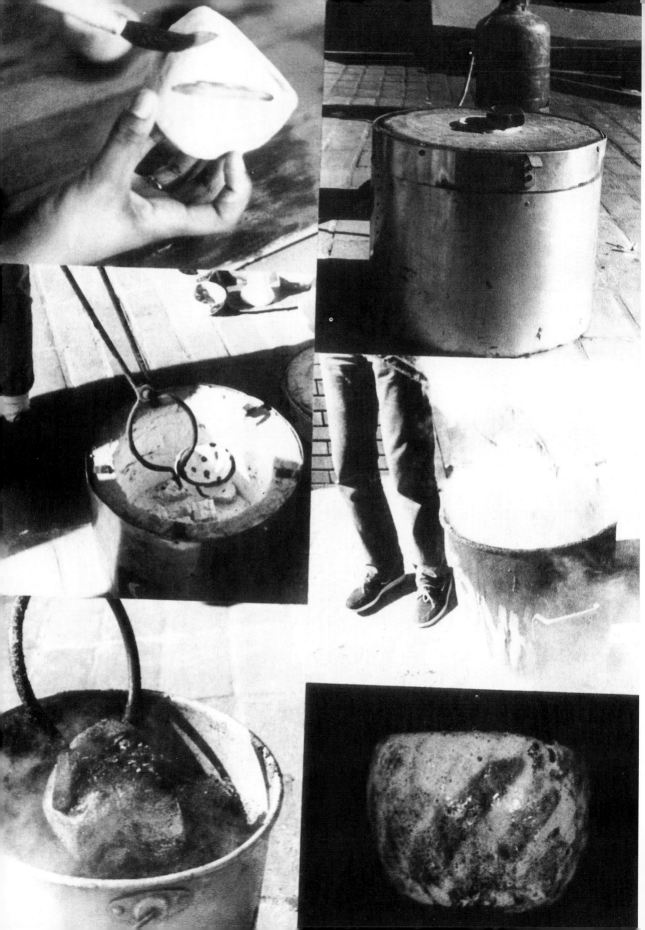

Raku – Happiness and a Method of Fast Firing

From Japan comes a way of firing pottery very quickly, perhaps taking only half an hour. This is the sort of firing used in tea ceremonies, where a guest is given a pinch pot to decorate and can then watch it being fired. As soon as it cools, the same pot can be used for drinking green tea in the ceremonial manner. The word raku means happiness in Japanese.

A pot for raku firing needs to be made of grogged or sand reinforced clay. After biscuit firing dip the pot into a special low temperature glaze and decorate it with brush painted oxides. The firing shown here uses a portable kiln lined with a heat retaining fibre blanket and using bottle gas. The kiln is very quickly heated up to red hot, then the pot is put inside using very long tongs and the lid is replaced.

As soon as the glaze has melted, which may take as little as 15 minutes, the pot is taken out again with the tongs and put into a metal bin full of sawdust, leaves or wood shavings. This produces flames and smoke, as you can see from the picture, but that is controlled by putting the lid on top of the bin. Then the flames stop because there is no more oxygen to feed them. After a few minutes the clay has become a rich black colour and the oxides changed into shining copper, gold or silver.

The pot can now be hunted out of the smouldering sawdust still using the tongs – rather like using a smoky lucky dip – and plunged into cold water before it is ready to use.

8 Potter's quiz

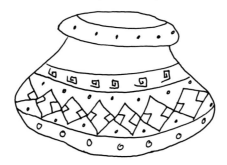

(the answers are given on the pages shown in brackets)

Where does clay come from?   (page 6)
What is an enemy to the potter's health?   (page 7)
What is the word for preparing a lump of clay?   (page 8)
What is the another name for a thumb pot?   (page 11)
What is a calabash?   (page 14)
How did Verona make her slab pot?   (page 17)
What would you use a template for?   (page 17)
What do you use to join slabs of clay together?   (page 17)
When is a pot leather hard?   (page 21)
How do you centre clay?   (page 23)
Can you remember four of the throwing tips?   (page 25)
What do you do with turning tools?   (page 26)
What is the foot of a pot?   (page 27)
What is the name of the brush used for sieving clay?   (page 37)
What is another word for glaze?   (page 49)
Name four materials from a glaze recipe.   (page 49)

What happens if you leave air in the clay?   (page 53)
What is the name for a potter's furnace?   (page 53)
How do pots kiss?   (page 53)
What can a dragon be used for in China?   (page 53)
In which country is there a special tea ceremony?   (page 57)
How did Sharon make her pot?   (page 59)
What is greenware?   (page 61)
What is a pyrometer for?   (page 61)

Can you think of any other questions?

Date   *Name*   *Score*

_____   _____   _____
_____   _____   _____
_____   _____   _____
_____   _____   _____

9 Pottery words and their meanings

Batt	a fireproof shelf to put aside the kiln
Biscuitware	(bisque) clay fired once
Body	the potter's word for clay
Cone	a tiny, long pyramid made of minerals like glazes, for measuring how the glaze is melting inside the kiln
Earthenware	low fired pottery, usually below 1100°C
Fettling	tidying up a pot when it comes out of a mould
Fireclay	a prefired and ground pottery material
Firing	cooking pottery in a kiln
Glaze	the glassy surface of a pot
Glaze firing	firing the pots again, this time covered with glaze
Greenware	unfired clay pots
Grogged clay	clay with grog or fireclay added
Impressed	pressing on to the clay surface to make a pattern
Incising	carving into clay to make a pattern
Inlay	a method of decorating a pot
Kiln	a potter's oven
Leather hard	stiff but not dry clay
Majolica	the name for a shiny white earthenware glaze
Mould	a plaster shape used in forming clay
Needle	a potter's hand tool with a thin point and a cork or wooden handle
Oxide	heat resistant pottery colours made from metals
Pugging	preparing clay in a pug mill
Pyrometer	what to use to measure the temperature of the kiln
Raku	a method of fast firing pottery
Sgraffitto	a way to decorate pots
Slab pot	a pot made by first rolling the clay out flat
Slip	liquid clay, often coloured with oxides
Slurry	clay that has been soaked down for using again
Stoneware	high fired pottery, usually above 1200°C
Tenmoku	the name for a rich, shiny black and brown stoneware glaze
Terracotta	brown coloured earthenware clay
Throwing	making a pot on the wheel
Thumb pot	a pinch pot made in your hand
Turning	trimming a pot when it is leather hard
Wedging	a way of preparing clay before use

10 More ideas

Books

BERENSOHN, P. *Finding One's Way with Clay: pinched pottery and the color of clay*, Simon and Schuster, 1972

BLANDINO, B. *Coiled Pottery: Traditional and Contemporary ways*, A. & C. Black, 1984

COLBECK, J. *Pottery: the technique of throwing*, Batsford, 1969

COOPER, J. *Pottery Decoration: contemporary approaches*, A. & C. Black, 1987

LEACH, B. *A Potter's Book*, Faber and Faber, 1940

MARSHALL, W. *Slab Building, Ceramic skillbooks*, A. & C. Black, 1982

Magazines

There are no pottery magazines just for children but these four for adults have lots of excellent photographs and would build into a good reference for you:

Ceramic Review
21 Carnaby Street
London W1V 1PH, England

Ceramics Monthly
Box 12448
Columbus, Ohio 43212, USA

Crafts
Dept CC
8 Waterloo Place
London SW17 4AT, England

Studio Potter
Box 70
Goffstown
New Hampshire, 03045, USA

Places to See Good Pots in the UK

Ashmolean Museum of Art and Archaeology
Oxford

Percival David Foundation of Chinese Art
53 Gordon Square
London WC1

Craftsmen Potters Shop
7 Marshall Street
London W1V 1FD

City Museum and Art Gallery
Bethesda Street
Hanley
Stoke-on-Trent, Staffs ST1 3DE

The Victoria and Albert Museum
National Museum for Art and Design
Cromwell Road
London SW7

Places to See Good Pots in the US

American Craft Museum
73 West 45th Street
New York NY 10019

Cooper-Hewitt Museum of
Decorative Arts & Design
Smithsonian Institute
9 E. 90th Street
New York NY 100193

Phoenix Art Museum
1625 North Central Avenue
Phoenix, Arizona

Buy Materials from here:

The Fulham Pottery
8–10 Ingate Place
London, SW8 3NS, England
Tel: 01 720 0050

Miami Clay Co.
270 N.E. 183rd Street
Miami, Florida 33179 USA
(305) 651–4695 Telex: 803208

Potterycrafts Ltd
Campbell Road
Stoke on Trent
Staffs, ST4 4ET, England
Tel: 0782 272444 Telex: 36167

American Art Clay Co. Inc.
4717 W. 16th Street
Indianapolis
IN 46222, USA

Moira Pottery Co. Ltd
Raw Materials Dept
Moira, Burton on Trent
Staffs, DE12 6DF, England
Tel: 0283 221 961

Minnesota Clay
8001 Grand Ave 50
Bloomington
Minn 55420
USA

Potclays Ltd
Brick Kiln Lane
Etruria
Stoke on Trent, England

Leslie Ceramics Supply Co.
1212 San Pablo Ave
Berkley
CA 94706, USA

Index

Where to Find Things in This Book